CW00819811

The Kids' Round the World Cookbook

Deri Robins

Illustrated by
Charlotte Stowell

Kingfisher Books

CONTENTS

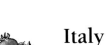

Kingfisher Books, Grisewood & Dempsey Ltd, Elsley House, 24-30 Great Titchfield Street, London W1P 7AD

First published in 1994 by Kingfisher Books
10 9 8 7 6 5 4 3 2 1
Copyright © Grisewood & Dempsey Ltd 1994
Illustrations © Charlotte Stowell 1994

All rights reserved. No part of this publication may be reproduced, stored in a retrieval system or transmitted by any means, electronic, mechanical, photocopying or otherwise, without the prior permission of the publisher.

BRITISH CATALOGUING IN PUBLICATION DATA
A catalogue record for this book is available from the British Library

ISBN 1 85697 286 0

Typeset by Tracey McNerney
Printed in Spain

Designed by Charlotte Stowell & Rob Howells
Cover design by Terry Woodley

GOOD COOK'S TIPS

We're about to set off on a whistle-stop tour of the world's best recipes! All you need is a kitchen, a friendly adult helper, and ingredients that can be found in most big supermarkets. Check you have everything you need before you begin!

Before you start, clean your hands and your work surface. It's also a good idea to clear up as you go along when you're cooking.

Make sure there's an adult in the kitchen. Someone should *always* supervise when you're chopping, blending or frying, or when you're taking things in and out of hot ovens.

Blenders make quick work of mixing liquids – but make sure the lid is on before pressing the switch!

Always use an oven glove when taking food from the oven. Put all hot pots and pans onto a trivet or a wooden chopping board.

Finally, mop up any spills immediately, before someone slips on them!

(Note: each recipe is enough for four people)

SCANDINAVIA

Sweden, Norway, Denmark, Finland and Iceland are all part of Scandinavia. There's a lot of coastline around these countries, so fishing is very important – fresh, smoked and pickled fish of all kinds are served up regularly!

Smørrebrød are little open sandwiches. You can use rye crispbreads, crackers or an ordinary sliced loaf.

SMØRREBRØD

Here are some typical Danish toppings:

Prawns, mayonnaise and hard-boiled eggs

Sliced or grated cheese with tomato and anchovies

Pâté topped with crispy bacon

Salami or cold ham with pickles

Sardines and cucumber

Or just use your own favourite toppings!

1 Butter several slices of bread. Arrange toppings on top, and decorate with some of the following.

2 Tomatoes – these look good if you cut them in a kind of zig-zag, as shown in the picture.

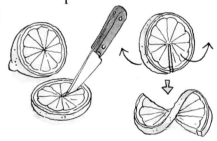

3 Cucumbers – run a fork down the sides before slicing, to make attractive flower shapes.

4 Lemon slices – these look pretty if you cut from the centre to the edge, and twist as shown.

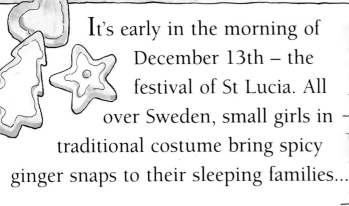

It's early in the morning of December 13th – the festival of St Lucia. All over Sweden, small girls in traditional costume bring spicy ginger snaps to their sleeping families...

GINGER SNAPS

You will need:
115g butter
115g brown sugar
1 egg white
200g plain flour
$\frac{1}{2}$ tsp bicarbonate of soda
1 tsp ground ginger

Set the oven to 180°C/ 350°F/gas mark 4.

1 Beat the sugar and butter until light and fluffy. Add the egg white, and beat well.

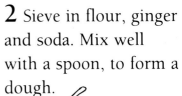

2 Sieve in flour, ginger and soda. Mix well with a spoon, to form a dough.

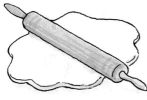

3 Sprinkle some flour onto your work surface, and roll out the dough carefully until it's about 6mm thick.

4 Use biscuit cutters to cut out shapes. Put them on a greased baking tray, and bake in the oven for ten minutes.

5 Try decorating the biscuits with icing sugar mixed with a little water and a drop of food-colouring.

NETHERLANDS

The Dutch are famous for their canals, their colourful tulips, their round, fat globes of Edam cheese – and their apple pancakes!

APPLE PANCAKES

You will need:
100g plain flour
Pinch of salt
300ml milk
1 egg
30g butter
3 large eating apples
1 tbsp water
Small bar of chocolate

1 Sieve the flour and salt into a bowl. Beat the egg and milk into the flour, to make a batter.

2 Peel, core and slice the apples. Put them in a pan with the water, and simmer for five minutes.

3 Melt a little butter over a gentle heat in a small frying pan. Pour in enough batter to cover the bottom.

4 Lift the pancake out when it's cooked on both sides. Pop it into a warm oven while you make the next one.

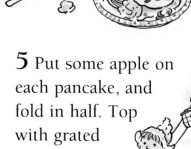

5 Put some apple on each pancake, and fold in half. Top with grated chocolate.

GREAT BRITAIN

In Britain today, Italian pizzas and Indian curries are as popular as roast beef and Yorkshire pudding! Here are three recipes that are both delicious *and* traditional...

ENGLISH SUMMER PUDDING

You will need:
500g mixed soft fruit
(raspberries,
strawberries,
blackberries,
blackcurrants, etc.)
125g caster sugar
About 6 slices of slightly
dry sliced white bread
1 tbsp water

1 Wash the fruit. Take out any stalks or pips. Put the fruit, sugar and water in a pan, and cook gently for three minutes.

2 Cut the crusts off the bread. Use all but one slice to line the bottom and sides of a 900ml pudding basin.

3 Fill the bowl with the cooked fruit, and make a lid from the last slice of bread.

4 Put a flat plate on top of the pudding, and press it all down with a heavy can.

5 Put it in the fridge overnight. Turn out onto a plate, and serve with yoghurt or cream.

SCOTTISH OATIE BISCUITS

If you thought that oats were just for making porridge with, think again...

You will need:
50g brown sugar
50g caster sugar
100g butter
2 tbsp golden syrup
75g plain flour
1 tsp baking powder
100g porridge oats
1 egg

Heat oven to 180°C/
350°F/gas mark 4.

1 Beat the butter with the sugars until light and fluffy. Add the egg and syrup, and mix well.

2 Sieve in the flour and baking powder, and add the oats. Stir until well mixed together.

3 Put heaped teaspoons of the mixture onto a greased baking tray, and flatten slightly.

4 Bake for 12 minutes, then lift onto a cooling rack. The biscuits will be slightly soft, but they'll become firm and chewy when they cool down.

LOCH NESS

8

WELSH RAREBIT
(sometimes called *Welsh Rabbit*)

There's no rabbit in this dish – just cheese, with a dash of milk and mustard!

People eat seaweed in many countries of the world. In Wales, a variety called Laver is turned into a kind of bread.

You will need:
4 slices of bread
3 tbsp milk
150g cheddar cheese
1 tsp mustard
Pinch of salt and pepper
Butter or margarine

1 Grate the cheese, and mix with the mustard and milk – this makes the 'rarebit'.

2 Toast each slice of bread lightly, and then take it out of the grill or toaster.

3 Butter the toast, and spread with the rarebit. Put under the grill until brown and bubbly.

GERMANY

There are well over a thousand different types of sausage made in Germany! They were originally made from wild boar (though most are now made from pork), and they are eaten at all times of the day...

To serve these dumplings at their best, leave them to cool down – then cut them into slices and fry in a little butter. They go well with any savoury dish.

BAVARIAN DUMPLINGS

You will need:
100g lean bacon
$\frac{1}{2}$ tbsp oil
6 slightly stale bread rolls (about a day old)
250ml milk
3 eggs
1 tbsp parsley
Pinch of salt and pepper

1 Cut the bacon into cubes. Heat the oil, and fry the bacon until golden brown.

2 Cut up the rolls, and put them in a bowl. Heat the milk, and pour over the bread.

3 Stir in the eggs, parsley, salt, pepper and bacon. With damp hands, form little balls from the dough.

4 Half-fill a big pan with water, and bring to the boil. Turn off the heat, and drop in the dumplings.

5 Leave for about 20 minutes – when they bob up to the surface, they're ready!

SWITZERLAND

Fondues are for sharing! Put the big dish in the middle of the table, and take turns to dip in bite-sized pieces of crisp vegetables and crusty bread...

SWISS FONDUE

You will need:

15g butter
1 clove garlic
1 tsp cornflour
300ml apple juice
240g Emmenthal
   cheese
240g Cheddar cheese
Salt and pepper
$\frac{1}{2}$ tsp ground
   nutmeg
Nice things to dip:
   chunks of apple,
   carrot, crisps, crusty
   bread, toast, etc.

1 Crush the garlic, and grate the cheese. Melt the butter, and cook the garlic for one minute.

2 Blend the cornflour with a little water. Add to the pan, along with the juice and cheese.

3 Cook over a low heat for five minutes, stirring with a wooden spoon. Add the nutmeg, salt and pepper.

4 Pour into an oven-proof dish. A food-warmer will keep the pot hot – but an adult *must* supervise.

FRANCE

French cooks always choose the very finest, freshest ingredients. They often cook them quite simply – as you'll see from the recipes shown here.

SALAD NIÇOISE

You will need:
2 eggs
4 tomatoes
4 spring onions
$\frac{1}{2}$ crisp lettuce
1 green pepper
200g can tuna in oil
50g French beans
50g can anchovies in oil
50g black olives

For the dressing:
4 tbsp olive oil
3 tbsp wine vinegar
1 clove garlic
Pinch of salt, pepper
  and caster sugar

1 Boil the eggs for ten minutes. Put in cold water until cool. Boil the beans for eight minutes, then drain them.

2 Slice the tomatoes, onions and pepper. Put them in a bowl with the beans and lettuce.

3 Drain and mash the tuna. Peel and slice the eggs. Arrange the eggs, tuna, anchovies and olives on the salad.

4 Peel and crush the garlic. Mix with the other ingredients for the dressing. Pour over the salad, and serve at once.

CHOCOLATE FROMAGE FRAIS

You will need:
200g milk chocolate
800g natural fromage
    frais

10g extra chocolate
(for decoration)

1 Break up the chocolate, and put it in a heat-proof bowl. Stand the bowl in a pan of boiling water.

2 Stir the chocolate until it melts, then leave it to cool. Fold it into the fromage frais.

3 Pour it into serving dishes. Top with extra fromage frais, and grate extra chocolate over the top. Chill for one hour.

4 If you prefer, you could flavour the fromage frais with orange or lemon juice (add honey or sugar to sweeten).

Snails in garlic butter are a big favourite in France. The French are so fond of these mouth-watering molluscs that some are specially bred on snail farms......

SPAIN

Paellas are cooked in all parts of Spain, but the ingredients can vary quite a lot from place to place. The usual rule is that whatever is freshest at market in the morning goes into the pot for supper!

PAELLA

You will need:
3 boned and skinned
  chicken breasts
$\frac{1}{2}$ green pepper
$\frac{1}{2}$ red pepper
1 clove garlic
1 onion
3 tbsp olive oil
280g long-grain rice
500ml water
397g can tomatoes
1 tsp turmeric
80g frozen peas
8 cooked prawns
8 cooked mussels
  (if you like them!)
  Pinch of salt
  Pinch of paprika
  1 lemon

1 Peel the garlic and onion. Take seeds and stalks out of the peppers. Chop them up. Slice the chicken into thin strips.

2 Heat the oil in a wide, shallow pan, and fry the chicken strips until they turn white. Add the chopped vegetables.

TAPAS are snacks served with drinks in Spanish bars. According to one story they were invented by a barman who used a slice of bread as a lid (a 'tapa') to keep flies off his customers' drinks!

14

3 Add the rice. Cook for a few minutes, stirring all the time.

4 Add the tomatoes, water, turmeric, salt and paprika. Simmer until the rice is cooked (about 15 minutes).

5 Stir in the peas, and lay the prawns and the mussels (if used) on top.

6 Cook for five more minutes, then serve with wedges of lemon.

15

ITALY

Italy has it all – beautiful countryside, great art, opera and football – and some of the most delicious food to be found anywhere on this planet...

PIZZA BASE

To make two bases, you will need:
1 tsp dried yeast
150ml warm water
250g plain flour
$^1/_2$ tbsp olive oil

1 Sieve the flour into a big bowl, and add the dried yeast.

2 Add the water and oil. Stir thoroughly until it forms a dough.

3 Knead until smooth and stretchy. Cover with a damp cloth, and leave to rise for 30 minutes.

4 Grease two round, 25cm baking trays. Halve the dough, and press each half into a tray.

5 Spread with your chosen toppings, and bake for 25 minutes at 180°C/350°F/gas mark 4.

TOPPINGS

One of the fun things about pizzas is that you can mix and match the toppings to your heart's content. Here are a few you might like:

For a basic pizza, spread tomato purée or home-made tomato sauce (see page 29) all over the dough. Top with grated cheese, some dried oregano and a few slices of tomato.

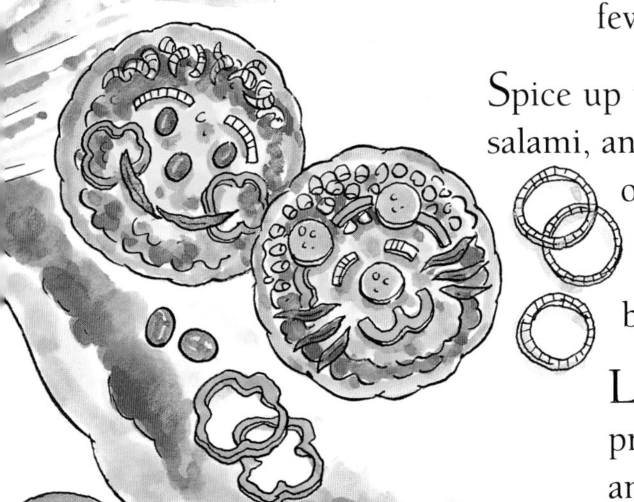

Spice up the tomato base with some sliced salami, anchovies, onion rings and a sprinkle of chilli powder...

For a breakfast with a difference, try adding bacon, fried egg and mushrooms...

Leave out the cheese, and add tuna fish, prawns (or any other shellfish), olives and red and green peppers, for a colourful, Mediterranean-style pizza.

PIZZA PARTIES

Treat your friends to a pizza party!
Make the bases before they arrive, and let them mix and match their own favourite toppings...

QUICK PIZZAS

Lightly toast some slices of bread, then cut into small circles with pastry cutters. Cover with your favourite topping, and put under a medium grill for a few minutes, until hot and bubbling.

GREECE

Although Greece and Turkey are two very different countries, they both share a lot of the same cooking ideas...

LAMB KEBABS

The lamb in this recipe is soaked in a special sauce called a marinade. (You can skip this stage if you like, but the meat won't be as tender.)

You will need:
4 tbsp olive oil
1 lemon
Pinch of salt and pepper
1 tsp dried oregano
700g lean lamb
1 onion
1 red pepper
1 green pepper

1 Squeeze the juice from the lemon. Mix with the oil, oregano, salt and pepper.

2 Cut the lamb into small cubes. Put it in the marinade, and leave overnight in the fridge.

4 Thread the lamb, onion and pepper onto skewers, as shown above.

5 Grill for 15 minutes, turning now and again until the meat is cooked.

It seems likely that the first kebabs were actually cooked by Turkish soldiers who used their swords as skewers!...

TURKEY

3 Peel and chop the onion, and cut the stalk and seeds from the peppers. Chop into small chunks.

Either serve the kebabs on the skewers with a helping of rice, or take them off the skewers and stuff into pitta breads, with some lettuce and sliced tomato...

HUMMUS

Chick peas and tahini can be bought in large supermarkets.

You will need:
175g can chick peas
4 tbsp tahini
2 lemons
2 garlic cloves
Pinch of salt
2 tbsp olive oil
Pinch of paprika

1 Peel and chop the garlic, and squeeze the juice from the lemons.

2 Put everything (except the paprika) into a blender, and blend it until smooth. Add a little water if you need to.

3 Pour onto a dish, and sprinkle with the paprika. Serve as a dip with pitta bread or vegetables.

For a simple, but always wonderful dessert, swirl a tablespoon of honey into a carton of Greek yoghurt and sprinkle with almonds.

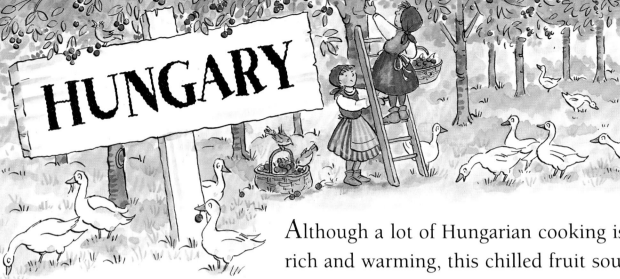

HUNGARY

Although a lot of Hungarian cooking is hot, rich and warming, this chilled fruit soup is also very popular.

COLD CHERRY SOUP

You will need:

*450g can stoneless cherries
  (you could also use
  raspberries or strawberries,
  if you prefer)*
125ml water
1 tbsp cornflour
25g sugar
1 tbsp lemon juice
Small carton soured cream
A few leaves of mint

1 Empty the can into a sieve over a pan. Press the cherries through the sieve (mash them in a blender first if this is difficult).

2 Add the water, and cook over a medium heat until the mixture starts to boil.

3 Mix the cornflour and sugar with a little water. Add this to the soup. Cook for ten minutes, stirring all the time.

4 Add lemon juice. Pour into a bowl, and put in the fridge to chill. Serve with a spoonful of cream and a few leaves of mint.

Large areas of Russia are covered by forest – so berry fruits, nuts and wild mushrooms all play a big part in the cooking.

Try serving this dish with boiled rice or noodles.

RUSSIA

To make home-made smetana, just mix 50g plain yoghurt with 50g of double cream.

SMETANA MUSHROOMS

You will need:
500g button mushrooms
50g butter
1 onion
I tbsp parsley
100g smetana (see above)
A pinch of salt and pepper

1 Wash and dry the mushrooms, and trim the ends off the stalks. Cut them in half, unless they are very small.

2 Melt half the butter in a frying pan. Cook the mushrooms for 15 minutes over a low heat, then spoon into a spare bowl.

3 Chop up the onion and the parsley. Put the rest of the butter in the pan, and fry them gently for ten minutes.

4 Drain the mushrooms, and add to the pan. Stir in the smetana, salt and pepper, and cook for five more minutes.

More sunflowers are grown in Russia than anywhere else in the world. The seeds are used in salads, or pressed to make oil and margarine.

INDIA

Many people in India never eat meat at all. As a result, a lot of the most interesting recipes are vegetarian.

STUFFED PARATHAS

Parathas are a kind of Indian bread. Here, they're stuffed with a mild vegetable curry.

For the stuffing:
2 large potatoes
100g white cabbage
250g can sweetcorn
1 tbsp olive oil
1 onion $^1/_2$ lemon
$^1/_2$ tsp garam masala
1 tsp ground coriander
$^1/_2$ tsp chilli powder
1 tsp sugar
Pinch of salt

For the parathas:
$^1/_2$ tbsp olive oil
$^1/_2$ tbsp butter
25g fresh mint leaves
$^1/_2$ tsp cumin
$^1/_2$ tsp chilli powder
1 tsp salt
1 tsp lemon juice
100ml water
300g plain flour

THE STUFFING

1 Peel the potatoes, and chop into small chunks.

2 Heat the oil, and fry the potatoes gently for a few minutes. Add 2 tbsp water, and cook until soft.

3 Chop the cabbage, and peel and chop the onion. Add to pan, and cook for another minute.

4 Mash or blend the corn, and squeeze the juice from the lemon. Add these to the pan.

5 Add the spices, salt and sugar, and mix well. Spoon into a bowl, and leave to cool.

THE PARATHAS

On really special occasions, paper-thin sheets of real gold and silver are used to decorate food, and are eaten as part of the meal....

1 Put the oil and butter in a pan, and heat gently until melted. Pour into a cup and leave to cool.

2 Put the mint, spices, salt, water and lemon juice into a blender. Blend for a few seconds.

3 Sieve the flour, and mix in the oil and mint sauce. Squelch it around until it makes a stretchy dough.

4 Sprinkle some flour onto your work surface, and divide the dough into eight balls.

5 Make a hole in the top of each ball, and spoon in a little of the curry mixture. Press the edges together.

6 Dust with flour, and roll out carefully until each ball is 12cm wide. Then put a heavy dry pan over a low heat.

7 Brush each paratha lightly with oil, and fry for a few minutes on each side, until big brown spots appear. Serve with raitha...

BANANA RAITHA

Spoon some plain yoghurt into a dish. Peel, trim and chop two spring onions, and add to the yoghurt. Peel and slice a banana, and mix this in too.

23

CHINA

A lot of Chinese food is fried very quickly over a high heat. Our recipe is full of all the right authentic Chinese flavours, but you can just pop it in the oven!

SOY CHICKEN WINGS

You will need:

2 tbsp soy sauce
1 tsp Chinese five-spice
1 tbsp lemon juice
2 spring onions
1 tbsp honey
1 tbsp tomato purée or ketchup
12 chicken wings
Some kitchen foil

1 Chop the onions. Mix with the soy sauce, spice, lemon juice, honey and tomato purée in a bowl.

2 Prick the chicken skin, and coat with the sauce. Cover, and leave overnight in the fridge.

3 Set the oven to 220°C/ 425°F/gas mark 7. Put the chicken wings on a sheet of kitchen foil on a baking tray. Keep the spare sauce!

4 Cook for about 45 minutes, turning them frequently and brushing with spare sauce. They should be crisp, brown and tender.

Chinese fishermen use specially trained cormorants to help them catch fish!

The Japanese eat rice with all their meals. Most homes have an electric rice cooker, so that there's a ready supply at all hours of the day!

JAPAN

VEGETABLE RICE

You will need:
3 tbsp olive oil
2 leeks
1cm root ginger
1 clove garlic
150g short grain rice
700ml water
Pinch of salt
250g green vegetables
  (try baby spinach,
   or frozen peas)

1 Wash, trim and chop the leeks. Peel and finely chop the ginger. Peel and crush the garlic.

2 Heat the oil in a wok or wide pan. Add the leeks, ginger and garlic, and fry gently for five minutes.

3 Add the rice, and stir for a few minutes. Add the water and the salt. Simmer for ten minutes.

4 Add the greens to the pan. Simmer for ten minutes, or until the rice is tender.

In Japan, food preparation is a real art. Raw fish and cooked rice are served in neat little packages called SUSHI, while vegetables are carved into all kinds of beautiful shapes.

25

INDONESIA & THAILAND

The spicy peanut sauce in this recipe is typically Indonesian. (You can also pour it over a bowlful of lightly cooked vegetables – this is called *Gado-Gado*.)

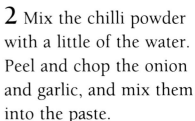

CHICKEN SATAY

You will need:

500g skinless, ready-boned chicken thighs
1/2 tsp chilli powder
1/2 tsp sugar
1 tbsp dark soy sauce
1 tbsp olive oil
1 onion
1 clove garlic
2 tbsp lemon juice
4 tbsp peanut butter
Pinch of salt
1 tsp ground cumin
1 tsp ground coriander
5 tbsp water

1 Cut the chicken into small chunks. Cook them just like kebabs (page 18) for eight minutes.

2 Mix the chilli powder with a little of the water. Peel and chop the onion and garlic, and mix them into the paste.

3 Heat the oil, and cook the onion mixture gently for five minutes. Add the rest of the ingredients, and stir well.

4 Serve the satays with the peanut sauce as a dip.

Coconuts are used a lot in Thai cookery. Monkeys are trained to collect them – they can manage around 500 on a good day!

CORN FRITTERS

In Thailand, vendors sell little fritters like these from stalls along the street.

You will need:
325g can sweetcorn
1 onion
$\frac{1}{2}$ tsp chilli powder
2 cloves garlic
1 tsp ground coriander
4 spring onions
3 tbsp plain flour
1 tsp baking powder
Pinch of salt
1 egg
4 tbsp olive oil

1 Drain the corn. Crush the kernels for a few seconds in a blender.

2 Peel and chop the garlic and onions. Mix with everything except the oil.

3 Heat the oil, and drop in a few teaspoonfuls of the mixture. Fry gently for three minutes, turn over, and repeat.

4 Drain on kitchen paper, and serve them while they're hot!

Boats laden with every imaginable type of food paddle along the floating markets of the Indonesian and Thai waterways...

27

USA

During the last century, millions of people from all over the world came to live in the USA. Today, American cooking is as rich and varied as the different nationalities who have made their homes here...

The birth of the Hot Dog (or, how the German sausage became an All-American treat): In 1906, an American cartoonist called Tad Dorgan was idly sketching as he watched a baseball game. He drew some frankfurters and made them look like dachshunds in buns. Underneath he wrote HOT DOGS...

CORNED BEEF HASH

Perhaps the ultimate brunch...

You will need:
4 medium potatoes
1 big onion
2 tbsp olive oil
450g can corned beef
Tomato ketchup

1 Peel and slice the potatoes. Put them in a pan, and cover with water. Bring to the boil, and simmer for 15 minutes.

2 Drain the potatoes, and fry them gently in half the oil until they're brown and slightly crispy all over. Take them out.

3 Peel and chop the onion. Put the rest of the oil in the pan, and cook for ten minutes.

4 Chop the corned beef, and mix with the onions, potatoes and ketchup. Heat through, and serve.

Fat orange pumpkins are sold in the autumn, and Pumpkin Pie is always a favourite at the Thanksgiving Day dinner in November.

PUMPKIN PIE

You will need:
A small pumpkin,
  weighing about 1.2kg
250g ready-made short
  crust pastry
300ml double cream
3 eggs
150g caster sugar
$\frac{1}{2}$ tsp salt
1 tsp ground ginger
1 tsp ground cinnamon
$\frac{1}{2}$ tsp ground nutmeg

Set the oven to 200°C/
400°F/gas mark 6.

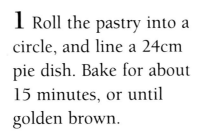

1 Roll the pastry into a circle, and line a 24cm pie dish. Bake for about 15 minutes, or until golden brown.

2 Scoop the flesh out of the pumpkin, and throw away the skin and seeds. Put in a pan, cover with water, and simmer for 25 minutes.

3 Drain away the water, and leave the pumpkin to cool down. Mash with a fork or in a blender until it's perfectly smooth and free of lumps.

4 Beat the pumpkin, eggs, cream, salt, sugar and spices. Pour into the pie dish, and bake at 190°C/ 375°F/Gas mark 5 for 40 minutes.

BEST EVER KETCHUP
Chop an onion, and fry gently in 1 tbsp oil for 5 minutes. Stir in 1 tbsp cornflour and cook for 2 minutes. Add a 397g can of tomatoes, 1 tbsp tomato puree, 1 tbsp fresh basil, 3 tsp brown sugar and a pinch of salt & pepper. Simmer for 5 minutes.

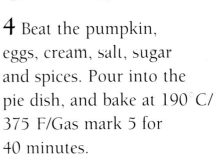

Serve with plenty of whipped cream!

HOLLYWOOD SALAD BOWL

The state of California has warm winters and long, hot summers. Salads and health foods are popular here – Californians like to keep themselves fit!

You will need:
1 crisp lettuce
1 avocado
1 orange
25g pecans or walnuts
3 tbsp mayonnaise
3 tbsp plain yoghurt
1 tbsp lemon juice
Pinch of salt and pepper

1 Wash the lettuce leaves, and drain them in a colander or salad spinner.

2 Peel the orange, and chop up the segments. Arrange on the lettuce.

3 Peel the avocado, and take out the stone. Chop into chunks, and sprinkle with lemon juice.

4 Add the avocado and the nuts to the salad.

5 Mix the mayonnaise and yoghurt with salt and pepper, and pour over the salad.

SURFER'S SHAKE

Delicious and nutritious!

You will need:
A big glass of milk
1 banana (or other soft fruit)

Throw all the ingredients in a blender. Switch on. Switch off. Drink.

CAJUN BREAKFAST SPECIAL

Down in Louisiana, the cooking has a spicy flavour – thanks mainly to the French, Spanish and Caribbean settlers who have made their home here.

New Orleans is world-famous for its jazz music, wild Marai Gras celebrations, and delicious cooking!

You will need:
200g stale bread
2 tbsp olive oil
1 onion
225g mushrooms
2 cloves garlic
1 stalk celery
4 sausages
6 rashers bacon
350g cheese
4 eggs
475ml milk
1 tbsp mustard
1 tsp cumin
1 tsp cayenne pepper

1 Grill the sausages and bacon under a medium heat until thoroughly cooked and brown.

2 Peel and chop the onion and the garlic. Wash and slice the celery and mushrooms.

3 Heat the oil in a pan. Cook the vegetables for five minutes over a medium heat.

4 Grate the cheese. Take crusts off the bread, and chop into cubes. Chop the sausages and bacon.

5 Put the bread into an ovenproof dish. Top with layers of sausage, bacon, cheese and fried vegetables.

6 Beat the eggs, milk and seasonings, and pour over the top. Cover the dish, and leave it overnight in the fridge.

7 The next morning, set the oven to 180°C/350°F/ gas mark 4. Take off the lid, and bake for one hour. Serve hot!

MEXICO

Spicy chillis carry a sting in their tails! Although some Mexicans like to chew the red-hot peppers *raw*, you'll find that a tiny pinch of chilli powder goes a very long way...

TORTILLAS

You will need: 200g wholemeal flour; 50g margarine or butter; 120ml warm water; some olive oil

1 Sieve the flour into a bowl. Add the margarine, cut up into pea-sized pieces, and stir in the water. Mix into a dough.

2 Divide into 12 balls. Brush with oil, cover with a cloth, and leave for 20 minutes. On a floured surface, roll into 14cm circles.

3 Brush a heavy pan with a tiny amount of oil. Cook the tortillas gently for two minutes on each side, until blisters appear.

4 Put a spoonful of your chosen filling in the middle of the tortilla, fold it over, and serve. Add some grated cheese.

HOT STUFF!

In Mexico there are over a hundred different kinds of chilli pepper – some hotter than others!

Did you know that chilli peppers, avocados, tomatoes, beans and TURKEYS all originally came from MEXICO?!!

Try filling your tortillas with some of these sizzling stuffings! Guacamole and salsa also make great dips for tortilla chips...

GUACAMOLE

You will need: 2 ripe avocados; juice from ¹/₂ lemon; 1 tomato; 1 spring onion; 3 tbsp soured cream; pinch of salt and chilli pepper

1 Chop up the spring onion. Peel and chop the tomato. Peel the avocados, cut in half, and take out the stones.

2 Mix all the ingredients together – either mash them up with a fork, or use an electric blender.

REFRITOS

You will need: 400g can red kidney beans; 1 onion; a clove of garlic; 30g margarine or butter; a pinch of chilli pepper

1 Peel and chop the onion and garlic. Melt the margarine in a pan over a medium heat, and fry the onion and garlic gently for five minutes.

2 Mash the beans, and add to the mixture with the pepper. Cook it all through until hot.

SALSA

You will need: 1 small can tomatoes; 1 small onion; chilli powder to taste (try ¹/₂ tsp); a pinch of sugar; a pinch of salt and pepper

The Mexican Day of the Dead is celebrated with all kinds of festive food – including little sugar skulls and skeletons!

Just peel and chop the onion, and mix it with the rest of the ingredients.

Cool down a hot salsa with a bowl of chilled soured cream and chopped cucumber!

CARIBBEAN

Next stop is the Caribbean – a group of tropical islands cradled between North and South America. Get ready for some sunshine cooking!

PINEAPPLE ICE-CREAM

You will need:
450ml milk
175g caster sugar
3 eggs
400ml double cream
Small can crushed
  pineapple

1 Beat the eggs, and mix them with the milk and sugar. Put the mixture in a saucepan.

2 Heat until the mixture starts to thicken. Beat with a whisk, and leave to cool down.

3 Whip the cream until it thickens. Fold the cream and crushed pineapple into the custard.

4 Pour the custard into a plastic container. Cover it, and put it in the freezer until firm.

These Caribbean vegetables can be cooked by peeling, chopping into chunks, and boiling in a pan of water until tender. Drain, and add a knob of butter.

ackee

breadfruit

sweet potato

cassava

In the tropical Caribbean climate, bananas grow all year round. They are more than just a food- for example the leaves are sometimes plaited together to make roofs.....

BANANA BREAD

You will never want to eat ordinary bread again...

You will need:
250g plain flour
1 tbsp baking powder
500g ripe bananas
125g butter
125g sugar
1 egg
1/2 tsp salt
1/2 tsp grated nutmeg
100g raisins
4 tbsp chopped pecans

Set the oven to 180°C/ 350°F/gas mark 4.

1 Beat the butter and sugar until light and fluffy. Add the egg, and beat thoroughly.

2 Sieve the flour, baking powder, salt and nutmeg into another bowl. Peel and mash the bananas in a third bowl.

3 Beat a little of the flour into the egg. Mix in a little banana. Repeat until flour and banana are used up.

4 Stir the nuts and the raisins into the batter. Scrape it all into a greased 1-litre loaf tin.

5 Bake for one hour. Use a knife to check that the middle is cooked – it should be clean when you pull it out.

AFRICA

As Africa is a great big continent with over 50 countries, it's hardly surprising that there's no such thing as a 'typical African meal'! Here's a slightly spicy dish from South Africa.

BOBOTIE

You will need:
1 onion
1 tbsp olive oil
2 slices bread
350ml milk
400g minced beef
1 tbsp curry powder
25g flaked almonds
50g raisins
1 tbsp lemon juice
Pinch of salt and pepper
2 eggs

Before you start, set the oven to 180°C/350°F/ gas mark 4.

1 Cut the crusts off the bread, break it into chunks, and soak it in half of the milk.

2 Chop the onion. Heat the oil in a pan, and fry the onion over a low heat for ten minutes.

4 Spoon the whole lot into an ovenproof dish. Beat the eggs with the rest of the milk, and pour over the mixture.

5 Put it in the oven for 1¼ hours. The top of the bobotie should be set and golden brown.

Peanuts are grown in many parts of Africa. Try making your own home-made peanut butter: Put 100g salted peanuts and 1 tablespoon of vegetable oil into a blender and switch on – the longer you blend, the less crunchy it will be.

3 Add the mince, curry powder, lemon juice, nuts, raisins, salt and pepper to the pan. Fry until the meat is brown all over.

BAKED BANANAS

African meals usually end with some fresh fruit, or a simply cooked dessert.

You will need:
4 large bananas
2 tbsp brown sugar
1 tsp cinnamon
30g butter or
  margarine

Set the oven to 180°C/ 350°F/gas mark 4.

1 Cut the bananas in half lengthwise. Put in an ovenproof dish, with the cut sides facing up.

2 Melt the butter in a pan over a low heat. Stir in the sugar and the cinnamon.

3 Pour over the bananas. Cover the dish with kitchen foil, and bake for 45 minutes.

AUSTRALIA

When the famous ballerina Anna Pavlova toured Australia, a leading chef was so bowled over that he invented this recipe in her honour. The meringues are said to resemble her swirling tutu!

PAVLOVA

You will need:

5 eggs
150g caster sugar
250ml double cream
350g creamy Greek
  yoghurt
1 small can pineapple rings
2 kiwi fruits
A few sprigs of mint
Non-stick baking paper

Heat the oven to 150°C/300°F/Gas mark 2 before you begin.

1 Cut a circle from the non-stick paper, using a big plate as a guide.

2 Crack the eggs, and separate the whites from the yolks. (Scramble the yolks for breakfast!)

3 Whisk the whites until they are stiff enough to stand up in peaks – an electric mixer is best for this.

Witchetty grubs are considered to be a great delicacy by some Aborigines. They are said to taste a bit like scrambled eggs.

The Koala bear is a very fussy eater. It will only eat the fresh young leaves from particular sorts of gum tree....

4 Gradually add the sugar, one tablespoon at a time. Whisk well before adding each new tablespoonful.

5 Spoon the mixture in a ring on the paper. Bake for five minutes, then lower the heat to 120°C/250°F/gas mark $\frac{1}{2}$.

6 Bake for 50 minutes, or until it's crisp on the outside. Leave to cool, then peel off paper.

7 Whisk the cream until slightly stiff, then fold in the yoghurt. Pile it in the middle of the ring.

8 Chop the pineapple and kiwi, and arrange on top of the cream. Decorate with sprigs of mint, and serve at once.

SPIDERS!

Fill a tall glass with fizzy cola or lemonade (or any other flavour).

Add a blob of ice-cream and a straw.

39

MIDDLE EAST

Middle Eastern cooking is colourful, rich, and scented with spices. It's a very hospitable part of the world, and food plays a big part in making visitors welcome.

BÖREK

You will need:
250g filo pastry
4 tbsp olive oil
350g feta cheese
Large bunch of mint
Pinch pepper and nutmeg

Heat the oven to 180°C/350°F/gas mark 4.

1 Crumble the feta cheese into a mixing bowl. Add the pepper and nutmeg.

2 Wash the mint, and cut up with scissors. Add to the cheese, and mash with a fork until creamy.

3 Take out the strips of filo. Cut them in half, so that each strip is about 7-8cm wide.

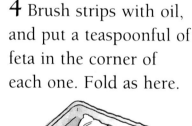

4 Brush strips with oil, and put a teaspoonful of feta in the corner of each one. Fold as here.

A typical Middle Eastern meal begins with a tableful of starters called 'mezze'. As well as the little pies shown here, you might be offered olives, pickles, nuts, salads and dips such as hummus (see page 19).

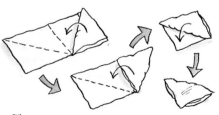

5 Keep folding, so that you end up with fat little triangles. Repeat until all the feta is used up.

6 Brush with oil, and bake on a greased baking tray for 25 minutes, or until golden.